FROM SEA to SHINING SEA

NEW HAMPSHIRE

TERRY MILLER SHANNON

Consultants

MELISSA N. MATUSEVICH, PH.D.
Curriculum and Instruction Specialist
Blacksburg, Virginia

ANN HOEY, M.A., M.S.I.
Youth Services Coordinator
New Hampshire State Library
Concord, New Hampshire

CHILDREN'S PRESS ®
AN IMPRINT OF SCHOLASTIC INC.

New York · Toronto · London · Auckland · Sydney · Mexico City
New Delhi · Hong Kong · Danbury, Connecticut

New Hampshire is in the north-eastern part of the United States. It is bordered by Maine, Vermont, Massachusetts, the Atlantic Ocean, and Quebec, Canada.

Project Editor: Meredith DeSousa
Art Director: Marie O'Neill
Photo Researcher: Marybeth Kavanagh
Design: Robin West, Ox and Company, Inc.
Page 6 map and recipe art: Susan Hunt Yule
All other maps: XNR Productions, Inc.

Library of Congress Cataloging-in-Publication Data

Shannon, Terry Miller, 1951-
    New Hampshire / by Terry Miller Shannon.
      p. cm. — (From sea to shining sea)
    Includes bibliographical references and index.
    ISBN-10: 0-531-21138-X
    ISBN-13: 978-0-531-21138-0
1. New Hampshire—Juvenile literature. I. Title. II. Series.

F34.3 .S53 2009
974.2—dc22

                                      2001007856

TABLE of CONTENTS

CHAPTER ONE

INTRODUCING THE GRANITE STATE

New Castle is a small New Hampshire community known for its beautiful homes and oceanside parks.

New Hampshire is a small, wedge-shaped state tucked into the northeastern corner of the United States. New Hampshire is so small that it is only a two-hour trip from the eastern border to the western border, and less than five hours from the northern border to the southern border. Only six other states are smaller than New Hampshire.

Despite its size, New Hampshire has great quantities of valuable natural resources. In fact, it is often called "the Granite State," after its most well-known natural resource. The speckled rock called granite appears everywhere in New Hampshire. It is under your feet, in walls, and in the mountains. Long ago, these granite deposits attracted European settlers who were interested in quarrying granite, which was used to construct buildings throughout the northeast.

New Hampshire also has many interesting people, places, and things, including:

- Picturesque small towns, old stone walls, and covered bridges
- The White Mountains, popular for camping and hiking
- Dozens of lakes, streams, and ponds for boating, swimming, and sailing
- Mount Monadnock, the most-climbed mountain in the world
- Strawbery Banke, one of New Hampshire's early settlements that is today an outdoor history museum
- Dartmouth College, one of the country's leading universities
- Mystery Hill in North Salem, where some of the oldest buildings in North America are located

New Hampshire is also associated with several famous people. Poet Robert Frost found inspiration in the state's beautiful scenery. Two other celebrated residents, Alan B. Shepard Jr. and Christa McAuliffe, made great strides in space travel. The fourteenth president of the United States, Franklin Pierce, was from New Hampshire.

New Hampshire is a land of scenic wonders, important historical events, and an independent spirit. Turn the page to discover the unique and very special state of New Hampshire.

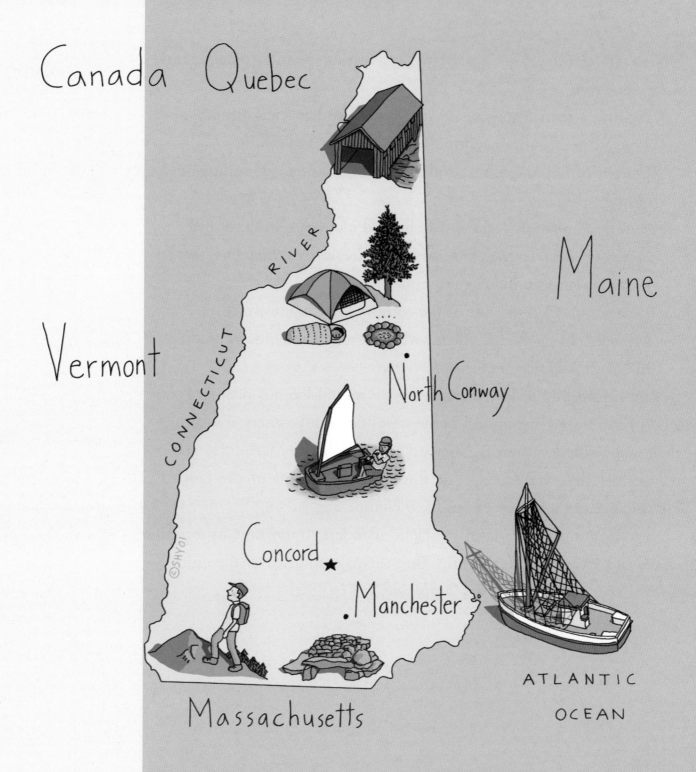

Canada Quebec

Maine

Vermont

CONNECTICUT RIVER

North Conway

Concord ★

. Manchester

©SHY01

Massachusetts

ATLANTIC OCEAN

CHAPTER TWO

THE LAND OF NEW HAMPSHIRE

New Hampshire is shaped like a roughly cut piece of pie, with the crust edge facing south. Maine and the Atlantic Ocean border the east. Massachusetts is to the south, and Vermont lies to the west. Quebec, a province of another country, Canada, edges the north.

Although the total area of New Hampshire is quite small—only 9,350 square miles (24,216 square kilometers)—the land is completely different from place to place. The state is flat near the seacoast, but otherwise hilly. It holds hundreds of lakes and ponds, and an abundance of forests filled with white pine, elm, maple, fir, and hemlock trees. Gentle, rolling hills are never far from towering mountains.

The land of New Hampshire was shaped by the last ice age, which ended about 10,000 years ago. Creeping sheets of ice called glaciers sculpted the earth by erosion, or the gradual wearing away of land, and

This photo shows a view of Mount Kearsarge in the White Mountains.

New Hampshire's White Mountains are a popular place for hikers and climbers.

FIND OUT MORE

Find out how the Ice Age changed the land. Soak a piece of sandstone in water overnight. Then freeze it overnight. What happened to the rock? Why?

by moving earth from one place to another. When glaciers moved across the continent they created the mountains and lakes that are part of New Hampshire today.

There are still ice age souvenirs throughout New Hampshire's landscape. The glaciers moved boulders and deposited them in areas with completely different rock types. These out-of-place boulders are called erratics. New Hampshire's Madison Boulder is one of the largest known glacial erratics in the world. In other places, curved hills such as Great Boar's Head in Hampton were pushed into shape by moving glaciers. These hills are known as drumlins. New Hampshire also has "kettle lakes" that were once holes underneath glaciers. When the glaciers melted, the holes filled with water and became lakes. Lake Winnipesaukee was formed by glaciers.

GEOGRAPHIC REGIONS

There are three land regions in New Hampshire: the Seaboard Lowland, the New England Upland, and the White Mountains.

Seaboard Lowland

The Seaboard Lowland is the coastal region in the southeast corner of New Hampshire. Of all the New England states that border the ocean, New Hampshire has the shortest coastline—only eighteen miles (29 kilometers) long.

The coast is lined with beaches. Inland bodies of water called estuaries contain a combination of fresh and ocean water. The ocean, coast, marshes, tidal pools, and estuaries are home to a variety of birds, fish, seals, whales, raccoons, beavers, and deer.

Off the coast of Portsmouth, there are nine islands called the Isles of Shoals. Four of the islands—Lunging, Star, Seavey's, and White—belong to New Hampshire; the others belong to Maine. A few people live on these rugged islands or spend summers there.

The rocky coastline of Star Island is typical of the rugged scenery on the Isles of Shoals.

New England Upland

The New England Upland covers the southern part of New Hampshire, except for the Seaboard Lowland near the coast. This region includes the Merrimack River Valley and the Connecticut River Valley.

The Merrimack River Valley is in the south central part of the state. Three of New Hampshire's largest cities are in the Merrimack River Valley—Manchester, Concord, and Nashua. The highway between Nashua and Concord is crowded with buildings and traffic, yet there are protected natural areas such as Beaver Brook Natural Area in Hollis. The area covers 1,700 acres (688 hectares) of forest, fields, and wetlands.

In Concord, you can stroll a 90-acre (36-ha) conservation center run by the Society for the Protection of New Hampshire Forests. Fertile farmlands also stretch alongside the Merrimack River.

The Connecticut River Valley is a narrow strip along the western border of New Hampshire, between one and two miles (2 and 3 km) long. Postcard-perfect church steeples dot the towns of the Upper Valley. Rolling hills and rich farmland are filled with fields of corn or grazing cows.

Farms dot the gently rolling hills of the Connecticut River Valley.

FIND OUT MORE

In early fall, tourists flock to the Connecticut River Valley to admire the brilliant red, orange, and yellow leaves. What causes the leaves to change color in the fall?

In the state's southwestern corner towers the giant Mount Monadnock. This granite mountain was formed long ago when glaciers wore down the area. Where did Mount Monadnock get its name? A monadnock is a single rock peak above a plain that remains after the surrounding land has been worn away by glaciers. Since the mountain is harder rock than the surrounding hills, less of it was scoured away. Although Mount Monadnock's height of 3,165 feet (965 meters) can't compete with the White Mountains, this mountain appears huge because it stands alone above rolling farmland, gentle hills, ponds, and streams.

In the area surrounding Monadnock, you're likely to see blackberry, raspberry, and blueberry bushes. Cardinals are attracted to the berries, and brilliant orange and black monarch butterflies spend summers in western New Hampshire. You may also see deer, moose, coyotes, raccoons, skunks, chipmunks, and cottontail rabbits.

New Hampshirites are careful to avoid moose even as they drive along the highways.

11

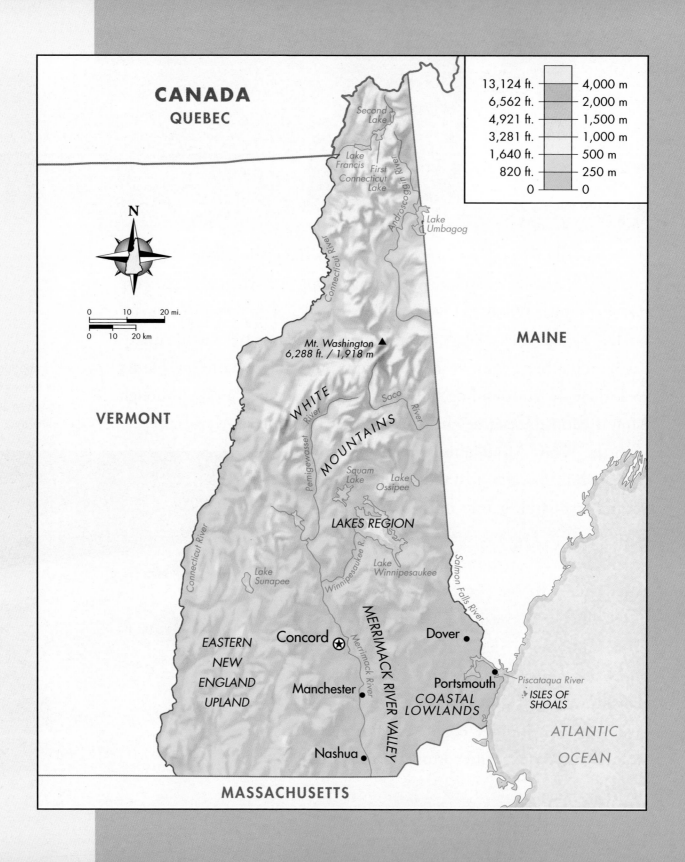

CANADA
QUEBEC

Second Lake

Lake Francis

First Connecticut Lake

Androscoggin River

Lake Umbagog

13,124 ft. — 4,000 m
6,562 ft. — 2,000 m
4,921 ft. — 1,500 m
3,281 ft. — 1,000 m
1,640 ft. — 500 m
820 ft. — 250 m
0 — 0

N

0   10   20 mi.

0   10   20 km

Connecticut River

MAINE

Mt. Washington ▲
6,288 ft. / 1,918 m

VERMONT

WHITE

Saco River

Pemigewasset River

MOUNTAINS

Squam Lake

Lake Ossipee

LAKES REGION

Connecticut River

Winnipesaukee R.

Lake Winnipesaukee

Salmon Falls River

Lake Sunapee

EASTERN
NEW
ENGLAND
UPLAND

MERRIMACK RIVER VALLEY

Dover ●

Concord ⬟

Merrimack River

Portsmouth ●
Piscataqua River

COASTAL
LOWLANDS

ISLES OF
SHOALS

Manchester ●

ATLANTIC

OCEAN

Nashua ●

MASSACHUSETTS

The White Mountains region includes the White Mountains in the north central part of the state as well as northern New Hampshire. The White Mountains are part of the Appalachian Mountain Range stretching from central Maine to Georgia. They may have been named "White Mountains" because of their snow-capped peaks.

Some of the White Mountains' granite ridges are called the Presidential Range because they are named after presidents. Mount Eisenhower, Mount Pierce, and Mount Jackson are part of the Presidential Range, as is Mount Washington, the highest mountain in the northeast. It stands 6,288 feet (1,918 m) high.

Valleys called notches have been carved through the White Mountains by glaciers. Notches often serve as passageways through the mountains. Crawford Notch and Franconia Notch are two notches that run through the White Mountains.

The White Mountain National Forest attracts tourists year round. The forest has more than one hundred waterfalls, dozens of lakes, and

Crawford Notch, shown here, is the main passage through the White Mountains.

13

many brooks and streams. The forest was once home to the Old Man of the Mountain, a rocky ledge that looked like a face. The famous face collapsed in 2003. Construction for the Old Man memorial began in 2007. Another popular attraction in White Mountain National Forest is the Flume, an 800-foot (244-m) granite canyon full of rushing water and hidden caves.

In northern New Hampshire there is a remote wilderness of mountains, forests, streams, and lakes that is sometimes referred to as "the North Country." It is the most remote part of New Hampshire. This area is thickly forested with spruces, hemlocks, firs, maples, and birches. Timber companies own most of the land in the North Country.

LAKES AND RIVERS

New Hampshire has about 1,300 lakes. The largest, Lake Winnipesaukee, covers about 70 square miles (180 sq km) and holds hundreds of small islands. Other New Hampshire lakes are Squam, Sunapee, Winnisquam, and Ossipee. Part of Lake Umbagog lies in Maine. River damming has created artificial lakes such as Franklin Falls Reservoir, Hopkinton Lake, Everett Lake, Edward MacDowell Lake, and Surry Mountain Lake.

The state also has a wealth of rivers. New Hampshire is sometimes called "The Mother of Rivers," because several rivers in the New England area originate in the White Mountains. The Connecticut River, New Hampshire's longest river, begins in the mountains and flows south

Lake Winnipesaukee is one of 273 lakes in what is known as the Lakes Region of New Hampshire.

through Massachusetts and Connecticut, emptying into the Long Island Sound. The Connecticut River serves as the border between New Hampshire and Vermont.

Other rivers include the Pemigewasset River, which begins at Profile Lake at Franconia Notch and flows south, joining with the Winnipesaukee River at Franklin to form the Merrimack River. The Merrimack River continues south into Massachusetts. The Androscoggin and Saco Rivers begin in northern New Hampshire and flow into Maine. In southeastern New Hampshire,

EXTRA! EXTRA!

In the early 1900s, several mills dumped waste into the Nashua River, which runs through New Hampshire and Massachusetts. As a result, the river became severely polluted. In 1962, local resident Marion R. Stoddart formed a group called the Nashua River Watershed Association to clean up the river. Her organization persuaded companies to stop dumping waste in the river and encouraged the building of waste treatment plants. The Nashua River is much cleaner today as a result of these citizens' efforts.

the Piscataqua and Salmon Falls Rivers are part of the New Hampshire–Maine border. They both empty into the harbor at Portsmouth.

CLIMATE

New Hampshire weather varies as much as its land. Changes in climate depend on proximity to the ocean and elevation. For example, in July, it might be snowing on Mount Washington while swimmers at the seashore are soaking up the sun. The temperature may also vary within the same area, especially in the mountains, where a pleasant summer day can turn to snow and ice in a short time.

In winter, there are long stretches of below-zero temperatures, and summers tend to be cool. The record high to record low temperature

The highest peaks of the White Mountains sometimes have snow even in the summer.

range of 106° Fahrenheit (41° Celsius) and −46°F (−43°C) is one of the most drastic for any state.

Wind and rain are not uncommon. New Hampshire receives rain in every season, with an average of about 42 inches (107 centimeters) per year. Wind in the mountains can be an awesome force. A world record-breaking wind of 231 miles (372 km) per hour was recorded at Mount Washington on April 12, 1934.

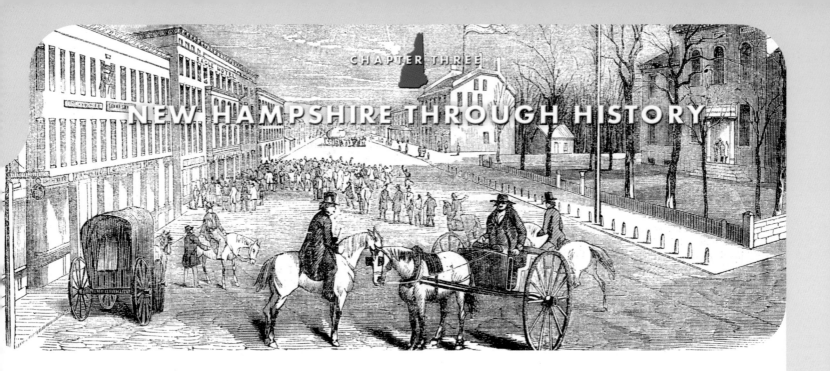

CHAPTER THREE

NEW HAMPSHIRE THROUGH HISTORY

This drawing shows the center of town in Concord in the early 1800s.

The first people to arrive in the area we call New Hampshire were nomads, or wanderers, who came to North America about 12,000 years ago. These Paleo-Indians relied on hunting for food and moved often to follow their food supply. Stone tools have been found throughout New Hampshire, providing evidence of these early people.

About 3,000 years ago, the descendants of these early people began living in villages. They learned how to farm, and grew corn and squash. They also acquired skills such as pottery making and woodcarving.

Before the Europeans arrived, about five thousand Native

EXTRA! EXTRA!

A mysterious site at North Salem offers a sign of the area's ancient residents. What has become known as Mystery Hill (also known as "America's Stonehenge") is a series of rock walls, tunnels, rooms, and wells covering thirty acres (12 ha). Scientists believe pottery pieces found at the site are about 3,000 years old. Mystery Hill has some of North America's oldest buildings. Scientists disagree as to what the structures may have been used for. Some say they were used to watch the stars, while others think they may have been used for religious sacrifices.

Americans lived in New Hampshire. Many Native Americans in the New England area (the northeastern United States) belonged to the Algonquian group. In New Hampshire, the Abenaki and Pennacook branches were part of the Algonquian culture and shared the same language. These groups included the Ossippe and the Pequawket (Abenaki), as well as the Nashua, Piscataqua, Souhegan, Amoskeag, and Squamscot (Pennacook).

Native Americans settled along the Connecticut, Saco, Androscoggin, and Merrimack rivers, as well as around the lakes and along the coast. They grew beans and corn, which was eaten whole or ground into cornmeal, and hunted wild birds and deer. They created paths and trails leading to places for fishing, hunting, and trading. They also traveled New Hampshire's rivers and streams to other settlements for trading.

Early Algonquians in New Hampshire built homes from bent saplings covered with reed mats.

John Smith was responsible for exploring much of the New England coast.

EARLY EUROPEAN EXPLORERS

English captain Martin Pring may have been the first European to explore New Hampshire in 1603. Pring soon returned home to report his findings. The next explorer was Samuel de Champlain from France. He arrived in 1605 and mapped the coast of New Hampshire, Maine, and Massachusetts.

Another Englishman, Captain John Smith, was hired by English investors to map the same area. In his notes to England he described the coastline as "the strangest pond I ever saw." England's King James was so impressed by Smith's maps and descriptions that he named the area New England.

After Smith's trip, the English government began giving out land grants in what became known as the New World. To accomplish this, a group called the Council for New England was formed in London, England in 1620. In 1622, the Council gave land to John Mason and Sir Ferdinando Gorges. Mason and Gorges were English businessmen and friends of John Smith. The land grant gave them all the land between the Merrimack and Kennebec rivers for 60 miles (97 km) inland.

THE NEW HAMPSHIRE COLONY

John Mason wanted to start colonies in the New World. He and Ferdinando Gorges formed The Laconia Company to settle the land along the Piscataqua River and to trade with Native Americans for furs. Mason named his land "New Hampshire" after England's Hampshire County.

In 1623, Mason sent a Scotsman named David Thomson to establish a fishing colony. Thomson's group of about a dozen explorers settled at the mouth of the Piscataqua River. They called New Hampshire's first settlement Little Harbor or Pannaway, which was later named Rye. At about the same time, another group settled eight miles (13 km) away in Northam, which later became Dover. King James provided assistance to the early colonies by sending supplies and giving away free land. In return, the settlers were loyal to England.

Most pioneers—usually city people—came in search of personal wealth, but were ill-prepared for the harsh life that awaited them. They had no experience in making a wilderness livable and productive. Fish and wild game were plentiful, but the settlers didn't know how to hunt. The weather was unfriendly. The soil was thin and rocky. It took about three years to make a small plot of land ready for planting. Trees had be cut and burned, and rocks had to be dug out by hand.

English investors at The Laconia Company became discouraged as they spent more and more money on the settlement. They sent food, tools, clothing, and fishing and building equipment to the settlers. They also sent guns and ammunition, animals and feed, and plants and seeds. In return, the English investors received only small shipments of animal furs, which they could sell for a profit. When the settlers sent ironstone from the White Mountains, however, the English were unimpressed.

Passaconaway was a leader of the Pennacook and a friend to the early settlers.

This drawing shows Ferdinando Gorges and John Mason naming the provinces.

With help from the Native Americans, settlers eventually learned to use the area's natural resources. Native Americans taught the settlers how to use herbs for medicine and showed them routes through the wilderness. Settlers learned how to trap animals and birds for food and clothing, which helped them to survive the harsh winters. To pay for the right to use land between the Piscataqua and Merrimack rivers, settlers gave the Native Americans clothing and kettles. The natives kept their right to fish, hunt, and plant in the area. When John Mason died in 1635 and The Laconia Company fell apart, the settlers divided the land and continued on.

EXTRA! EXTRA!

Early settlers found a plentiful supply of tall, straight white pine trees in northern New Hampshire. Trees of this size were scarce in England. Because they were perfect for building ship masts, King James claimed them for use in making English navy ships. He sent surveyors to the area to mark the biggest, strongest trees, and imposed fines on anyone who was caught cutting them down. This was the start of the shipbuilding industry in New Hampshire.

By 1640, more settlers arrived, and the population in New Hampshire was almost a thousand. Colonists settled the Piscataqua River and the coast towns of Strawbery Banke (later called Portsmouth), Dover, Exeter, and Hampton. They were mostly involved in fishing, furs, or timber. They lived in log cabins, and built meeting houses and mills to cut wood and grind grain.

By now, the citizens of New Hampshire needed a system of government. Borrowing an idea from the English government, a community of "towns" was created and declared a royal province of England in 1679. In 1698, New Hampshire was governed by Massachusetts until 1741, when the two colonies were separated, but still under English control.

Although the two colonies were now separate, no official boundaries had been declared. New Hampshire and Massachusetts argued over land ownership until 1741, when its southern and eastern boundaries were officially fixed. In 1764, the king announced that the Connecticut River would serve as New Hampshire's western border.

Other boundaries were in question, as well. In the colony's early years, Native Americans and settlers were friendly neighbors. As more and more newcomers settled in New Hampshire, however, they took over land that belonged to Native Americans and relations between the two groups worsened. They fought over land rights. Also, the settlers built river dams to power mills and sailed English ships in the rivers, making it difficult for Native Americans to fish. Logging drove animals far into the woods, making it just as difficult to hunt. In addition, many Native Americans had no resistance to diseases such as smallpox that had been brought by the settlers. By 1700, thousands of Native Americans had died from smallpox and other diseases, leaving very few remaining in New Hampshire.

THE FRENCH AND INDIAN WAR

News of the successful New Hampshire colony attracted the French, as well as the British. French-speaking hunters and trappers moved into the area from Quebec and France.

Great Britain and France fought bitterly over North American lands. The French were mainly interested in trading with natives for furs, while the British wanted to make New England their home. In 1754, war broke out between France and Britain. The French and Indian War (1754–1763) was mostly fought by attacking enemy forts in unsettled areas. Many Native Americans sided with the French for fear that the British would take more of their land. They also attacked settlers' homes.

A New Hampshire man named Robert Rogers formed the Rangers, a group of New Hampshire spies and scouts who worked for the British. The Rangers destroyed the home base of a group of enemy Native Americans. Other New Hampshire soldiers also cap-

The French and Indian War was fought between the French and the British to gain control of North America.

tured enemy camps. In 1763, a peace treaty was signed, giving half of North America, including all French claims east of the Mississippi River, to Britain.

After the war, life was good throughout the colony. New towns were established and old towns grew. In 1719, a group of Scots-Irish from Londonderry, Ireland, moved into the Merrimack River Valley in south central New Hampshire. They made linen fabric in a town they named Derry. The port town of Portsmouth prospered. It developed into a bustling shipping center and became the main hub of New Hampshire's industries, selling lumber and pine masts. The people in Portsmouth were merchants, shipbuilders, and lumbermen.

Portsmouth was a busy cultural and industrial center in the 1700s.

FIND OUT MORE

About 1733, both New Hampshire and Massachusetts claimed ownership of a town called Rumford. In 1741, King George II gave the town to New Hampshire and it was renamed Concord. Look up the word *concord* in the dictionary. How does the meaning of the word apply to the situation between New Hampshire and Massachusetts?

Dr. Wheelock and his family gathered in prayer at the site of Dartmouth College.

The royal colony flourished under the leadership of one of the most important families in New Hampshire, the Wentworths. King George I of Britain appointed John Wentworth first lieutenant governor of New Hampshire in 1717. His son, Benning Wentworth, became the first independent governor in 1741. Benning Wentworth worked to separate New Hampshire from the Massachusetts Bay Colony. His generous system for giving land to people helped settle the colony's interior.

In 1769, his nephew, Sir John Wentworth, gave land to a minister named Eleazar Wheelock to build New Hampshire's first college, Dartmouth College. Wheelock had a special interest in educating Native Americans, and his new school was meant for both colonists and Native Americans.

Located in Hanover, Dartmouth (named after the Earl of Dartmouth) became a hub for brilliant minds. Many famous people graduated from the college, including some of New Hampshire's early governors, soldiers, clergy, and politicians. The school attracted educated people to the area, and roads and inns were built to accommodate them. It wasn't long before Hanover developed into a small, bustling city.

THE RISE OF A REVOLUTION

By the time Sir John Wentworth became royal governor in 1770, many colonists were unhappy with their ties to Great Britain. The French and Indian War had been expensive, and to raise money Britain imposed taxes (extra charges) on products sold to the colonies, including tea and paper. The colonists were furious. They felt that the taxes were illegal because the colonies were not represented in British government. The phrase, "No taxation without representation" became their slogan. Colonists were also required to give British soldiers food, shelter, and supplies, but they resented having British royal forces within their territories.

Gradually, tension between the two sides increased. On December 14, 1774, New Hampshirites attacked Fort William and Mary, a British fort at New Castle. They took weapons and ammunition without firing a shot. It was one of the very first acts of the American Revolution (1775–1783). Governor Wentworth was humiliated. Despite his best efforts, hundreds of New Hampshirites fought for the colonies' independence when the war began in April 1775.

WHO'S WHO IN NEW HAMPSHIRE?

Daniel Webster (1782–1852) was one of America's best-known lawyers and orators (speakers). He represented New Hampshire in the United States House of Representatives and the Senate, and he also served as secretary of state under three presidents. Webster was born in Salisbury (now Franklin) and graduated from Dartmouth College.

WHO'S WHO IN NEW HAMPSHIRE?

John Langdon (1741–1819) was a sea captain, shipbuilder, and merchant. He led the raid on Fort William and Mary and signed the United States Constitution on behalf of New Hampshire. He later became one of the first United States senators to represent the state (1789–1801) and served as governor of New Hampshire four times (1785–1786; 1788–1789; 1805–1809; 1810–1812). He was born near Portsmouth.

On January 5, 1776, New Hampshire became the first colony to adopt a constitution, a document that stated the basic principles and laws of the future state, and outlined citizens' rights. On July 4, 1776, all thirteen colonies approved the document called the Declaration of Independence. Three men from New Hampshire—Matthew Thornton, William Whipple, and Josiah Bartlett—signed on behalf of the colony.

Although no battles took place in New Hampshire, New Hampshirites fought elsewhere in every major battle for independence. In August 1777, New Hampshire general John Stark led 1,500 soldiers to defeat the British at the Battle of Bennington in Vermont.

In 1783, the colonies won the war and gained their independence from Britain. On June 21, 1788, New Hampshire was the ninth state to ratify (accept) the United States Constitution, a document that out-

Many New Hampshirites participated in the Battle of Bennington, which was actually fought in Walloomsac, New York, several miles west of Bennington, Vermont.

lined how the government of the United States would be organized. New Hampshire's vote put the Constitution into effect.

In 1775, New Hampshire's capital was moved from Portsmouth to Exeter. After the American Revolution, state lawmakers met in eight different towns to avoid showing favoritism to one area of the state. Finally, in 1808, Concord was chosen as the new capital.

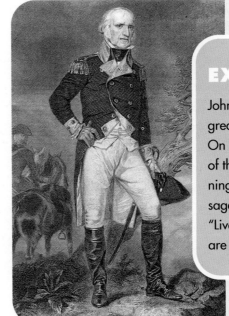

EXTRA! EXTRA!

John Stark was New Hampshire's greatest Revolutionary War hero. On the thirty-second anniversary of the victory at the Battle of Bennington, John Stark sent a message to veterans of the conflict: "Live free or die." Those words are now the state motto.

In the early 1800s, New Hampshire life revolved mainly around farming. However, it was a struggle to grow crops on the hilly, rocky, thin soil, and the state's severe weather made for a short growing season. Farmers worked with hand tools like hoes, rakes, and axes, and used lots of muscle. Women worked at least as hard as the men to clothe, feed, and care for their children. They helped with farm chores and made butter and fabric to sell. Shoes were made at home. Trading goods and services with neighbors was the only way to survive.

New Hampshirites had fun, too. They blended enjoyment with work through church meetings, quilt-making parties, and county fairs. When a farmer needed a new barn, he invited his neighbors to a "barn raising." Huge meals were served as the whole community gathered to help. The barns were built quickly thanks to the contribution of many hands.

EXTRA! EXTRA!

A religious group called the Shakers moved to America in the late 1700s. They were nicknamed Shakers because they shook, shouted, and danced as part of their religious ceremonies. Several Shakers settled north of Concord in Canterbury Shaker Village, where they grew their own food and made their own necessities. In the mid-1800s, Canterbury had more than 300 Shakers. Today, there are few Shakers left in the United States. Canterbury Shaker Village is open to visitors interested in learning about the lifestyle and values of the Shakers.

In 1790, about 142,000 people lived in New Hampshire. By 1850, the population had climbed to 318,000, but was growing slowly. Many people left New Hampshire looking for cheap, rich land elsewhere that was easier to farm.

FROM FARMING TO MANUFACTURING

In the late 1800s, New Hampshire became less agricultural and more industrial. People left farms to work in the textile mills and shoe factories that started in New Hampshire cities. In 1840, half of New Hampshire's land was used for farming. By 1870, farmers used less than four in every ten acres (1.6 in every 4 ha).

Over time, community life revolved around the mill. In Manchester, the Amoskeag Manufacturing Company was one of the world's largest textile (cloth) mills, turning out four million yards of fabric each week. The mill, which employed 17,000 people by the turn of the century, built houses for its workers and donated land for community cultural centers.

Millwork, however, was difficult. In the Amoskeag Mill, the noise of the weaving looms was described as so loud it was "fright-

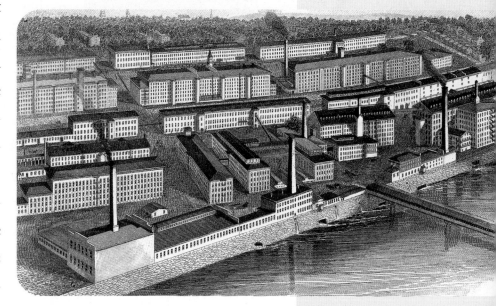

The Amoskeag Mill was once one of the largest textile factories in the world.

This drawing shows a woman working at a loom in a textile mill.

ful." The room was filled with dust and tiny bits of cotton that damaged workers' lungs. The windows were kept closed, and it was hot. Girls who lived in mill housing usually slept two in a bed, with three beds in each room. It was common to work a 13-hour day. New Hampshire was the first state to pass a law that required workdays to be less than ten hours.

The mills brought in thousands of workers from other countries. Starting in 1840, Irish, English, French, German, Scottish, Swedish, Russian, and Greek workers moved into the area from their native countries. Most of the mill workers were from French Canada.

CIVIL WAR

By 1848, the United States was arguing bitterly over slavery. In colonial days, Africans were shipped to the colonies and sold into slavery. Enslaved Africans were forced to do backbreaking labor on farms. They did not have the freedom to go where they wanted, and were often not allowed to learn how to read and write. Enslaved Africans were used mainly in the South to work on large farms called plantations.

Some enslaved Africans were used in New Hampshire until the late 1700s. In 1779, after the American Revolution, nineteen enslaved Africans asked the New Hampshire House of Representatives for freedom. They argued that since American patriots were asking for freedom from Britain, it was only fair to give freedom to enslaved Africans, as well. Lawmakers said no to their plea, but some New Hampshire slavers freed their enslaved Africans. In 1790, there were 158 enslaved Africans in New Hampshire. By 1820, there were 786 free African Americans in New Hampshire and no one was enslaved.

New states joined the country as either a "free" state (where slavery was illegal) or a "slave" state. The South wanted new states to permit slavery, and the North wanted new states to be free states. To ease the tension between North and South, New Hampshire senator Daniel Webster helped to pass a series of acts called the Compromise of 1850. As part of the Compromise, California was admitted as a free state, but a law was passed to make sheltering an escaped African a crime, even in the free states.

In the meantime, some New Hampshirites, along with other Northerners, helped enslaved Africans to escape from the South through the Underground Railroad. The Underground Railroad was not an actual railroad, but a group of people who helped fleeing Africans make their way to

EXTRA! EXTRA!

Prince Whipple was an enslaved African owned by wealthy New Hampshirite William Whipple. When Captain Whipple went to fight in the American Revolution, he tried to take Prince with him. It is said that Prince told General Whipple, "You are going to fight for your liberty. But I have none to fight for." The general agreed to free Prince in exchange for his help fighting. During the war, Prince Whipple worked for General George Washington, who later became the first president of the United States.

WHO'S WHO IN NEW HAMPSHIRE?

Franklin Pierce (1804–1869) was the only United States president from New Hampshire (1853–1857). He served as president during a period of increasing tension between North and South. Although he was a firm supporter of the United States government, he also supported the South's pro-slavery stance. Pierce was born in Hillsboro.

freedom in Canada or the northern United States. The "conductors" hid people in safe spots known as "stations." The runaways mostly moved at night from station to station.

In 1861, Abraham Lincoln, who was against slavery, became president. Shortly after he was elected, the southern states began to secede, or leave, the United States to protect their right to enslave Africans, among other things. In February 1861, the southern states formed a new government and a new nation called the Confederate States of America.

Tensions ran so high between North and South that the Civil War began (1861–1865). On April 12, 1861, Confederates fired on the Union troops at Fort Sumter in Charleston, South Carolina. New Hampshire soldiers fought on the Union side, with about 36,000 men serving. In April 1865, the Union won the Civil War and slavery ended. Freed Africans became United States citizens.

GROWTH AND CHANGE

After the war, New Hampshire's fabric and shoe industries prospered. Settlements in Keene, Claremont, Nashua, Somersworth, Dover, Exeter, and Lebanon developed into mill towns as thousands of people moved in to work at the mills.

After 1850, railroads were the most important form of transportation in New Hampshire. Train tracks were everywhere, with 893 miles (1,437 km) of track laid down by 1874. Trains took farm products to cities and carried manufactured goods to rural areas. Mountain railroads carried lumber. The railroads also carried tourists, as people flocked to see New Hampshire's mountains, lakes, and trees. Huge, elegant hotels sprang up along the coast and in the White Mountains.

In the last half of the 1800s, lumber became a moneymaking business. Although there had been small lumber mills in New Hampshire's North Country since 1825, they grew after the Civil War. Brown Company, in Berlin, was the largest lumber mill. The Brown Company once owned 6,000 square miles (15,540 sq km) of land in Maine, Vermont, and New Hampshire—an area larger than the state of Connecticut.

Partly because it was easier to haul logs out of northern New Hampshire's forests on the railroads, lumber companies began to strip the forests of trees. They moved into an area and stayed until all the trees were cut, then they moved on. Without trees, rain and wind eroded (wore away) the soil. Branches and underbrush that were left behind sometimes fed huge forest fires. The severe logging, forest fires, and erosion destroyed much of northern New Hampshire's forests.

As a result of the widespread destruction, the United States government created the White Mountain National Forest in 1911. No one could cut trees in the park without permission from the government. Creation of the park was the first of many efforts to save and protect New Hampshire's land.

A NEW CENTURY

In 1917, the United States entered World War I (1914–1918) in Europe. Germany, a country involved in the war, was fighting with a new weapon—submarines. Ships had no defense against them. The Germans' sudden submarine attacks angered many Americans, including United States President Woodrow Wilson, who called it "warfare against mankind." Not only did more than 20,000 men from New Hampshire fight in the war, but the shipyard at Portsmouth began building and repairing war ships and submarines.

After the war, New Hampshire's fabric industry nearly died. In the 1920s, local mills struggled to compete with mills in southern and midwestern parts of the United States where people worked longer hours for less pay. Mill owners cut wages and increased workloads. In 1922,

Mill workers, many of whom were children under sixteen, worked long hours. These workers are leaving at the end of a shift.

Amoskeag Manufacturing Company decreased wages and increased working hours.

These changes made mill work even more difficult. To protect their rights, mill workers joined together in unions. Unions protected workers by bargaining for higher wages and shorter working hours for all members of the union. When mill owners at Amoskeag Mills refused their demands, workers went on strike and refused to work. Although they went back to work after nine months, it was the beginning of the end for cloth

FAMOUS FIRSTS

- The first potato was planted in the United States in Derry, 1719
- New Hampshire was the first state to declare freedom from Britain, 1774
- New Hampshire was the first state to create a revolutionary constitution, 1776
- Levi Hutchins of Concord invented the first alarm clock, 1787
- The first free U.S. public library was established in Peterborough, 1833
- Alan Bartlett Shepard Jr. of East Derry was the first American to travel in space, 1961

manufacturers in New Hampshire. Mills lost the struggle to compete with those in the South and many of them shut down. Unemployed mill workers moved away. New Hampshire's mill towns were extremely poor during the 1920s and 1930s.

Between 1929 and 1939, New Hampshire, along with the rest of the United States, entered the Great Depression. When the stock market crashed in 1929, many people lost money on their business investments and could no longer afford to buy products. As a result, factories closed down and thousands of people lost their jobs. The Great Depression was a terrible blow to New Hampshire. Even the Amoskeag Mill closed down in 1936, leaving 11,000 people without work.

To help put people back to work, President Franklin D. Roosevelt started the Civilian Conservation Corps (CCC). The CCC employed thousands of people to fix school buildings, plant trees, and build roads and dams. In New Hampshire, workers built country trails, roads, and picnic areas.

Even with Roosevelt's help, however, the 1930s was a time of struggle for New Hampshirites. They suffered a flood in 1936 and a hurricane in 1938 that caused millions of dollars in damage.

WHAT'S IN A NAME?

Some names of places in New Hampshire have interesting origins.

Name	Comes From or Means
New Hampshire	Hampshire County, England
Lake Sunapee	Native American words for "wild goose" (suna) and "lake" (nipi)
White Mountains	Sailors spotting chalky mountains with snowy peaks may have named these
Kancamagus Highway	Native American chief Kancamagus
Derry	Londonderry, Ireland
Mascoma Lake	Algonquian for "fish" (namas) and "water" (com)
Androscoggin River	Algonquian for "fish-curing place"
Piscataqua River	Native American for "where three rivers make one"

NEW HAMPSHIRE DURING WORLD WAR II

The start of World War II (1939–1945) helped bring the United States out of the Great Depression. The United States entered the war in 1941. New Hampshire products were once again in demand, as the Portsmouth Naval Shipyard set to work building submarines and warships. About 20,000 New Hampshirites worked in the shipyard. About 60,000 joined the United States armed forces. Thousands of other people found jobs in factories building weapons and supplies.

The USS *Albacore*, built in Portsmouth, was launched during World War II.

In 1944, as the war was coming to an end, world leaders gathered at Bretton Woods in New Hampshire's White Mountains. To repair wartime damage, they needed to find a way to simplify the transfer of money and expand trade between nations. It was at this meeting that an organization called the International Monetary Fund was created. This organization still operates today.

MODERN NEW HAMPSHIRE

When World War II ended in 1945, so did many jobs in war-related industries. Textron, a large textile mill in Nashua that made parachutes during the war, decided to close its doors in 1948. Suddenly, one in every three people in Nashua was out of work. To save their city, residents formed the Nashua, New Hampshire Foundation. The foundation bought vacant mills and found businesses to fill them. Newspapers and magazines called Nashua "the town that refused to die."

Limited money in the state meant that the New Hampshire government couldn't give much money to public education. In an effort to raise money, New Hampshire promoted itself as a vacation spot, hoping to attract tourists. Also, a state lottery, or sweepstakes, was started in 1964 to raise money for schools.

In the 1970s, the state's population skyrocketed at a rate twice the national increase. The state's rapid growth may have been partly due to its improved highway system. In 1956, New Hampshire, along with the other states, received money from the United States government to build highways. New Hampshire's roadways made traveling easier, and it wasn't long before tourism became a major business.

Because highways between New Hampshire and neighboring states were also improved, it became easier to live in New Hampshire and drive to neighboring states for work. Many chose to have a summer home in New Hampshire, with seashore and mountains just a few hours apart. Some moved to quiet New Hampshire to have a simpler lifestyle.

By this time, most New Hampshirites no longer worked on farms or in mills. They now worked in small manufacturing businesses, making products. Electronics industries (making television and computer parts, among other things) became a large part of the state's manufacturing business.

Once a struggling mill town, Nashua is now a busy, successful city.

SOLVING PROBLEMS

New industries brought conflict. Environmental battles began in the 1970s. In 1974, New Hampshire citizens successfully fought Aristotle Onassis, a rich businessman who wanted to build an oil refinery in Durham. The locals also fought against building a nuclear-power plant at Seabrook, but lost the fight. The plant opened in 1990.

People surged into New Hampshire in the 1990s, as more and more businesses opened. Most were high-technology firms that made medical equipment and computer software. Some old mill buildings now held modern electronics industries making parts for stereo, television, and telephone systems. These businesses attracted so many people that, at the beginning of 2000, about six in every ten New Hampshirites were originally from somewhere else.

The old Amoskeag Mill buildings now hold modern businesses such as DEKA, an electronics and software company.

In the late 1990s, New Hampshirites began to argue whether they should pay taxes on the money they earned. New Hampshire never had an income tax, but some residents thought that money generated from income taxes would help improve schools, which needed cash for teachers and supplies. Others, however, did not want to start paying the tax. In 1999, it was decided that the state would not collect income taxes.

An unlikely issue arose between New Hampshire and Maine in 2000. The two states have long disagreed over where the coastal border lies, and both states wanted to claim Portsmouth Harbor, which holds

Portsmouth Naval Shipyard. In Maine's view, the border is in the middle of the Piscataqua River. New Hampshire believes that the border is the Maine shoreline. In June 2000, the United States Supreme Court ruled that the Portsmouth Naval Shipyard is, in fact, in Maine.

Today, New Hampshire has a bright future. Residents and visitors alike value the state's high quality of life and its unique sense of place. It is likely that New Hampshire will continue to attract independent people and diverse industries for many years to come.

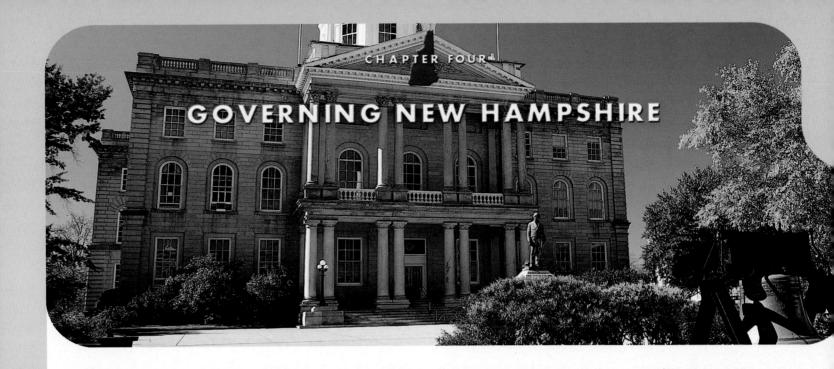

CHAPTER FOUR

GOVERNING NEW HAMPSHIRE

New Hampshire's constitution, which took effect in 1784, is the oldest in the United States. A constitution is a written plan of how the state will be governed. Although the New Hampshire constitution used today is essentially the same as it was in 1784, it has been amended, or changed, over time. Every seven years, the people vote to decide if the constitution needs to be changed. Two in every three voters (a majority) are required to pass constitutional revisions called amendments.

The three divisions, or branches, of government in New Hampshire are the executive, legislative, and judicial. The executive branch enforces and carries out laws. The legislative branch creates the laws. The judicial branch uses a court system and judges to interpret the meaning of laws.

A replica of the Liberty Bell sits on the capitol grounds in Concord.

EXECUTIVE BRANCH

The governor, elected for a two-year term, is head of the executive branch. He or she is in charge of overseeing New Hampshire's government. The governor has the power to call up the state's military forces in case of war or other emergency. He or she can also veto (reject) a bill before it becomes a law. However, a majority of the state's legislators (lawmakers) can vote to override the governor's veto.

An executive council, commonly known as the governor's council, has five members who assist the governor. They meet in the State House in Concord. These executive officers are elected every two years, and each member represents a certain area of New Hampshire. They are responsible for approving state office leaders and judges. They also assist the governor in many matters, including problems involving public waterways and the sale and purchase of land. The governor's council may also vote to reject the governor's actions.

LEGISLATIVE BRANCH

New Hampshire's state legislature, called the General Court, is one of the largest lawmaking (legislative) bodies in the English-speaking world. The legislative branch is divided into two sections: the house of representatives and the senate. Members of both houses write and pass New Hampshire's laws, including laws regarding taxes, education, transportation, and crime.

NEW HAMPSHIRE GOVERNORS

Name	Term	Name	Term
Meshech Weare	1784–1785	Natt Head	1879–1881
John Langdon	1785–1786	Charles H. Bell	1881–1883
John Sullivan	1786–1788	Samuel W. Hale	1883–1885
John Langdon	1788–1789	Moody Currier	1885–1887
John Pickerning (acting)	1789	Charles H. Sawyer	1887–1889
John Sullivan	1789–1790	David H. Goodell	1889–1891
Josiah Bartlett	1790–1794	Hiram A. Tuttle	1891–1893
John T. Gilman	1794–1805	John B. Smith	1893–1895
John Langdon	1805–1809	Charles A. Busiel	1895–1897
Jeremiah Smith	1809–1810	George A. Ramsdell	1897–1899
John Langdon	1810–1812	Frank W. Rollins	1899–1901
William Plumer	1812–1813	Chester B. Jordan	1901–1903
John T. Gilman	1813–1816	Nahum J. Batchelder	1903–1905
William Plumer	1816–1819	John McLane	1905–1907
Samuel Bell	1819–1823	Charles M. Floyd	1907–1909
Levi Woodbury	1823–1824	Henry B. Quinby	1909–1911
David Morrill	1824–1827	Robert P. Bass	1911–1913
Benjamin Pierce	1827–1828	Samuel D. Felker	1913–1915
John Bell	1828–1829	Rolland H. Spaudling	1915–1917
Benjamin Pierce	1829–1830	Henry W. Keyes	1917–1919
Matthew Harvey	1830–1831	John H. Bartlett	1919–1921
Joseph M. Harper (acting)	1831	Albert O. Brown	1921–1923
Samuel Dinsmoor	1831–1834	Fred H. Brown	1923–1925
William Badger	1834–1836	John G. Winant	1925–1927
Isaac Hill	1836–1839	Huntley N. Spaulding	1927–1929
John Page	1839–1842	Charles W. Tobey	1929–1931
Henry Hubbard	1842–1844	John G. Winant	1931–1935
John H. Steele	1844–1846	Henry Styles Bridges	1935–1937
Anthony Colby	1846–1847	Francis P. Murphy	1937–1941
Jared W. Williams	1847–1849	Robert O. Blood	1941–1945
Samuel Dinsmoor, Jr.	1849–1852	Charles M. Dale	1945–1949
Noah Martin	1852–1854	Llewelyn Sherman Adams	1949–1953
Nathaniel B. Baker	1854–1855	Hugh Gregg	1953–1955
Ralph Metcalf	1855–1857	Lane Dwinell	1955–1959
William Haile	1857–1859	Wesley Powell	1959–1963
Ichabod Goodwin	1859–1861	John W. King	1963–1969
Nathaniel S. Berry	1861–1863	Walter R. Peterson, Jr.	1969–1973
Joseph A. Gilmore	1863–1865	Meldrim Thomson, Jr.	1973–1979
Frederick Smyth	1865–1867	Hugh Gallen	1979–1982
Walter Harriman	1867–1869	Vesta M. Roy (acting)	1982–1983
Onslow Stearns	1869–1871	John H. Sununu	1983–1989
James A. Weston	1871–1872	Judd Gregg	1989–1993
Ezekiel Straw	1872–1874	Steve Merrill	1993–1997
James A. Weston	1874–1875	Jeanne Shaheen	1997–2003
Person C. Cheney	1875–1877	Craig Benson	2003–2005
Benjamin F. Prescott	1877–1879	John Lynch	2005–

New Hampshire legislators have been meeting in Representatives Hall for more than 190 years, making it the oldest chamber in the United States still in continuous use.

The House of Representatives has 400 representatives, while the state senate has 24 senators. Two representatives and two senators are elected to the United States Congress. New Hampshirites are proud of what they call "citizen legislature." Its legislators aren't professional politicians, but New Hampshirites from all occupations. As a result, they approach laws from the viewpoint of the people. Since there are so many legislators—about one for every 2,000 New Hampshirites—people always know who is representing them.

EXTRA! EXTRA!

New Hampshirites elected the state's first female governor, Jeanne Shaheen, in 1996, and reelected her in 1998 and 2000. At the same time, Donna Sytek was elected Speaker of the House (1996). She was also the first woman to hold that position, which requires her to preside over house meetings.

JUDICIAL BRANCH

The judicial branch interprets the laws, or decides what they mean. It is made up of four levels of courts: the supreme court, superior courts, district courts, and small claims courts. The governor and executive council select the judges for each court.

This photo shows the New Hampshire supreme court in session.

New Hampshire's supreme court is the highest court in the state. It decides if the lower courts applied laws correctly and fairly. The supreme court hands down final decisions on many civil, criminal, and juvenile cases. One chief justice (judge) and four associate justices make up the supreme court.

Each county has a superior court where jury trials are held. Superior courts hear civil cases involving divorce, custody, and real estate, as well as trials on major

EXTRA! EXTRA!

Since 1952, New Hampshire has been the first state to vote in the U.S. presidential primary. The presidential primary is an election that determines who will run for president and vice-president from each political party (Democratic and Republican). Winners of each party's election go on to run against each other in the general election. Many people think that New Hampshire's vote in the primary may influence other states' votes or even predict the way the nation will vote. For that reason, candidates tend to visit, hold meetings, and advertise in New Hampshire before their party's presidential primary.

NEW HAMPSHIRE STATE GOVERNMENT

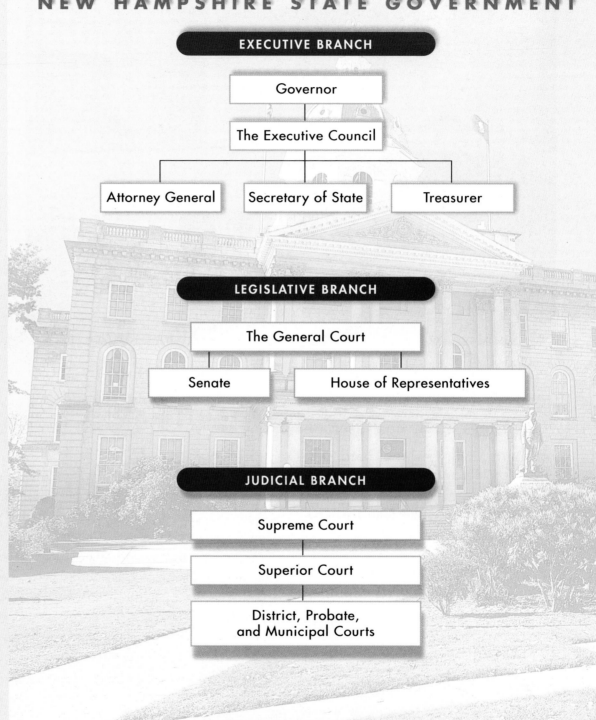

EXECUTIVE BRANCH

Governor

The Executive Council

Attorney General | Secretary of State | Treasurer

LEGISLATIVE BRANCH

The General Court

Senate | House of Representatives

JUDICIAL BRANCH

Supreme Court

Superior Court

District, Probate, and Municipal Courts

crimes. There are also more than forty district courts in New Hampshire. District courts hear minor cases such as traffic violations or cases involving less than $20,000.

TAKE A TOUR OF CONCORD, THE STATE CAPITAL

The city of Concord lies along the Merrimack River, above Manchester. More than 40,000 people live in Concord. It is not only the political center of the state, but also an industrial and commercial city.

The highlight of Concord is its gold-domed capitol, called the State House. When it was built in 1816, citizens donated land and granite for the building. Prisoners worked the granite into blocks. Oxcarts hauled the blocks to the site. When the capitol was finished in 1819, other businesses and homes were attracted to the area. It was remodeled in the 1860s and again in 1910. Today, you can tour the same room the legislature has met in since 1819.

Across the street from the state house is the Museum of New Hampshire History. The museum has many exhibits about the his-

Although Concord is a city, people live in close-knit neighborhoods. There are ten neighborhoods throughout the city.

Concord Coaches were popular because of their durability. They could roll over rough roads without breaking down.

tory of the state, such as the Concord Coach. These four-wheel carriages were first made in Concord in 1827. For seventy years they were widely produced and used throughout the American West. The museum also has the oldest dugout canoe in New England. Native Americans made the canoe from a hollowed-out log sometime between 1430 and 1660.

Also in Concord is the Pierce Manse, home of Franklin Pierce, fourteenth president of the United States. You can tour the home during certain times of the year. Or, you can visit Pierce's last resting place at Old North Cemetery. Some graves in the cemetery date back to the 1730s.

Christa McAuliffe Planetarium, located north of the downtown area, was built to honor the Concord teacher killed in the explosion of the

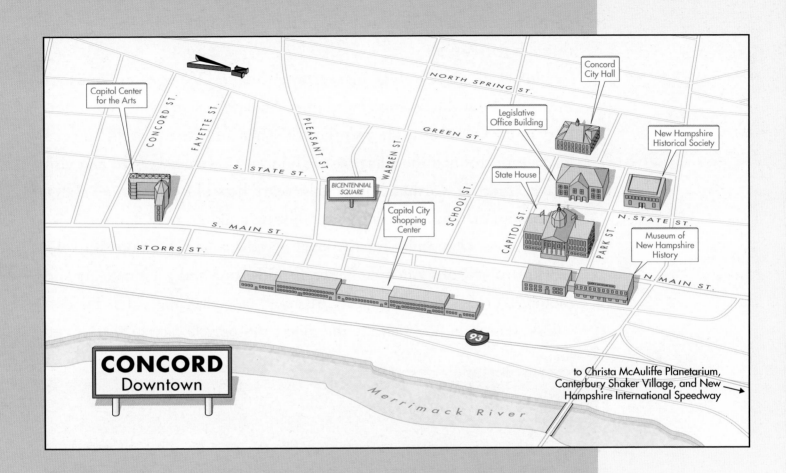

Capitol Center
for the Arts

Concord
City Hall

Legislative
Office Building

New Hampshire
Historical Society

CONCORD ST.

FAYETTE ST.

PLEASANT ST.

NORTH SPRING ST.

GREEN ST.

WARREN ST.

State House

S. STATE ST.

BICENTENNIAL
SQUARE

SCHOOL ST.

CAPITOL ST.

N. STATE ST.

PARK ST.

Museum of
New Hampshire
History

Capitol City
Shopping
Center

S. MAIN ST.

STORRS ST.

N. MAIN ST.

93

CONCORD
Downtown

Merrimack River

to Christa McAuliffe Planetarium,
Canterbury Shaker Village, and New
Hampshire International Speedway

FIND OUT MORE

Astronomy is the science of the stars and other heavenly bodies. An astronaut is a person trained to travel in space. What does the prefix "astro" mean?

space shuttle *Challenger*. At the planetarium, you can watch a show that makes you feel like you are blasting through outer space. You can also participate in activities such as building a rocket or viewing stars through telescopes.

North of Concord is Canterbury Shaker Village, an outdoor museum about the Shaker community. Shakers began living in Canterbury in the late 1700s. They worked the farm and ran sawmills. You can take a tour through the village to see how crops were harvested and visit Shaker places of worship. You can also learn how old-time Shaker crafts, like broom making, spinning yarn, and rug making, were done.

The New Hampshire International Speedway is in Loudon, 14 miles (23 km) north of Concord. Between mid-April and October, car and motorcycle races, including NASCAR races, take place there. The Loudon Classic started in 1923 and is the oldest motorcycle race in the United States.

At Canterbury Shaker Village you can tour some of the 25 original Shaker buildings.

54

CHAPTER FIVE

THE PEOPLE AND PLACES OF NEW HAMPSHIRE

New Hampshirites enjoy their independent, tough, and thrifty image. Much of that reputation probably came from their past. From the storming of Fort William and Mary during the Revolutionary War to toughing it out in farms and mills, New Hampshirites have always been people who could take care of themselves, even with few resources.

The Mount Washington Hotel opened in 1902 and was the most luxurious hotel of its day.

MEET THE PEOPLE

In 2005, New Hampshire's population was 1,309,940. Only nine states have fewer people. Between 1990 and 2000, New Hampshire added 11 people for every 100 people in the state. It was the fastest-growing eastern state north of Delaware.

55

Half of New Hampshire's residents live in cities, mostly in the south and southeast. Nearly one in every five New Hampshirites lives in Portsmouth, Dover, or Rochester (the Piscataqua River Valley). About one in every three residents lives in Manchester, Nashua, or Concord (the Merrimack Valley). Connecticut Valley cities, such as Keene, Lebanon, and Claremont, are smaller.

More than nine in every ten New Hampshirites are of European descent, and almost two in a hundred are Hispanic. About one in every one hundred is Asian. Less than one in every one hundred people is African-American or Native American.

WORKING IN NEW HAMPSHIRE

Many traditional New Hampshire industries (shoemaking, fabric industries, and others) have decreased over the years, replaced by tourism and high-technology industries. High-technology jobs include computer-related businesses, such as the manufacture of computers and computer parts, as well as electronic equipment, which includes medical machines, stereo systems, and televisions. The Merrimack Valley is crowded with high-technology and electrical industries.

Tourism is now one of the state's largest industries. Visitors come to New Hampshire year round to ski, hike in the mountains, stroll along the seashore, and admire the autumn leaves. In 2005, tourism generated about $5.6 billion for the State. People who work in tourism may run a hotel or motel, or plan and lead tours, among other things.

In the late 1800s, thousands of French-Canadians came to New Hampshire to work in its mills and factories. Today, many New Hampshirites claim a French-Canadian ancestor, and some people even speak French in addition to English. The French call French toast *pain perdu*, which means "lost bread." It's a thrifty and delicious way to use leftover bread, and a great excuse to have some tasty New Hampshire maple syrup. Remember to ask a grown-up for help!

USE-IT-UP, MAKE-IT-DO, FRANCO-AMERICAN TOAST

   4 eggs
   1 cup milk
   1 teaspoon vanilla
   1/2 teaspoon cinnamon
   8 slices day-old bread

1. Preheat oven to 500°.
2. In a medium-size bowl, beat together eggs, milk, vanilla, and cinnamon.
3. Place bread in a rimmed baking sheet.
4. Pour egg mixture over bread. Let stand five minutes.
5. Place greased cookie sheet in oven for five minutes to heat.
6. Carefully arrange bread slices on hot cookie sheet.
7. Bake for 8-10 minutes on each side or until nicely browned. Serve with butter and maple syrup. Serves 4.

There are about 100 lumber mills in New Hampshire.

Lumbering is a big industry in the North Country. In 1999, about 5,000 people worked in lumbering in New Hampshire. Lumbering jobs include cutting trees, driving logging trucks, and working in mills to produce lumber and wood products.

About 400 New Hampshirites work in the state's small mining industry digging out granite, gemstones, sand, and gravel. Gemstones are used in jewelry. Granite, sand, and gravel are used in building materials.

Less than one percent of New Hampshirites are farmers. There are about 3,600 farms in New Hampshire totaling about 400,000 acres (161,874 ha). Farmers and ranchers produce dairy foods, plants, fruits, vegetables, and maple syrup products. They specialize in producing blueberries, raspberries, maple syrup, dried flowers, and Christmas trees. They also raise beef, sheep, lambs, pigs, and chickens. Most farms are in the southern part of the state.

A large portion of the population works in the service industry. Nearly one in every three workers is a service worker, including teachers, janitors, police officers, firefighters, lawyers, and mechanics.

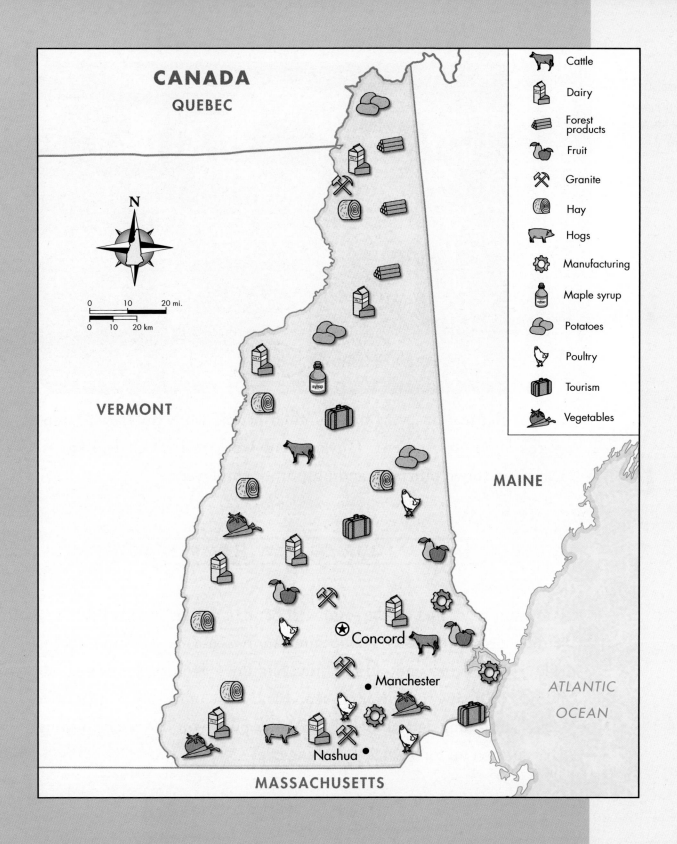

CANADA

QUEBEC

N

0   10   20 mi.

0   10   20 km

VERMONT

MAINE

MASSACHUSETTS

ATLANTIC OCEAN

★ Concord

Manchester

Nashua

Cattle
Dairy
Forest products
Fruit
Granite
Hay
Hogs
Manufacturing
Maple syrup
Potatoes
Poultry
Tourism
Vegetables

More than 40 million gallons of milk are produced on dairy farms in New Hampshire.

Almost fourteen in every one hundred people work for New Hampshire's large government. Government workers include legislators, selectmen (town officials), and post office employees.

TAKE A TOUR OF NEW HAMPSHIRE

The Seacoast

Portsmouth, located on the southwest bank of the Piscataqua River, is a harborside city on New Hampshire's short coastline. Portsmouth has cobblestone streets and old red brick buildings. Houses that were built in the 1800s now contain small shops, and tours of historic homes offer a peek into long-ago households. At the port, you can watch fishing boats or sign up for a whale-watching trip.

Strawbery Banke Museum is an outdoor museum that recreates life in a New Hampshire neighborhood more than three hundred years ago. The museum holds 42 buildings and several gardens. You can watch demonstrations of old-time crafts, such as boatbuilding and pottery making. The Children's Museum of Portsmouth has hands-on art and science displays. Visitors can climb into space shuttles and submarines, or watch shows about earthquakes and lobster catching.

Not far from Portsmouth are other attractions. Water Country, south of Portsmouth, is one of the largest water parks in New England. Northwest of Portsmouth is the rural town of Durham, home of the University of New Hampshire. More than 12,000 students attend the college, which frequently hosts arts-related events such as concerts and art exhibits.

The Merrimack River Valley

The Merrimack River Valley is in south central New Hampshire. The state's three largest cities are located here: Manchester, Nashua, and Concord. More than 107,000 people live in Manchester, the financial center of New Hampshire. You can wander among the old brick mill buildings that now hold modern businesses. The huge buildings of what used to be Amoskeag Mill stretch along the eastern banks of the Merrimack River. Industry is important here, including high-tech electronics, chemical plants, and warehouses. Manchester Airport is the state's largest airport.

Many old buildings in Manchester, such as these on Elm Street, house modern businesses.

Nashua, New Hampshire's second-largest city, has about 86,000 residents. Although there are more than 60,000 businesses in Nashua, many people who live there commute to work in Boston, Massachusetts, only 34 miles (55 km) away. A large number of shoppers come into Nashua from Massachusetts since there is no sales tax and several malls. If you're not in the mood to shop, explore the 800-acre (324-ha) park system. Many parks have swimming pools, ice-skating rinks, tennis and basketball courts, and playgrounds.

In the nearby town of Derry, you can explore poet Robert Frost's farm. Many of Frost's poems describe the life and landscape of New Hampshire and other New England states. You can learn more about Robert Frost at the farm, then walk the same trails he walked through in nearby forests and fields.

The Lakes Region

The Lakes Region revolves around Lake Winnipesaukee, New Hampshire's largest lake. The lake attracts thousands of visitors every year.

63

Weirs Beach is a lakeside beach town offering a boardwalk, arcades, and boat trips.

The town of Wolfeboro, on the southeast corner of Lake Winnipesaukee, claims to be America's first resort town. Even today, it is popular with tourists. Wentworth State Beach offers a shore for swimming and picnicking. In downtown Wolfeboro, you can walk the Russell C. Chase Bridge-Falls Path to see waterfalls. If you see a building with a tank "crashed" through the front

Because about one-fifth of Wolfeboro is water, it is a great place for water-related activities.

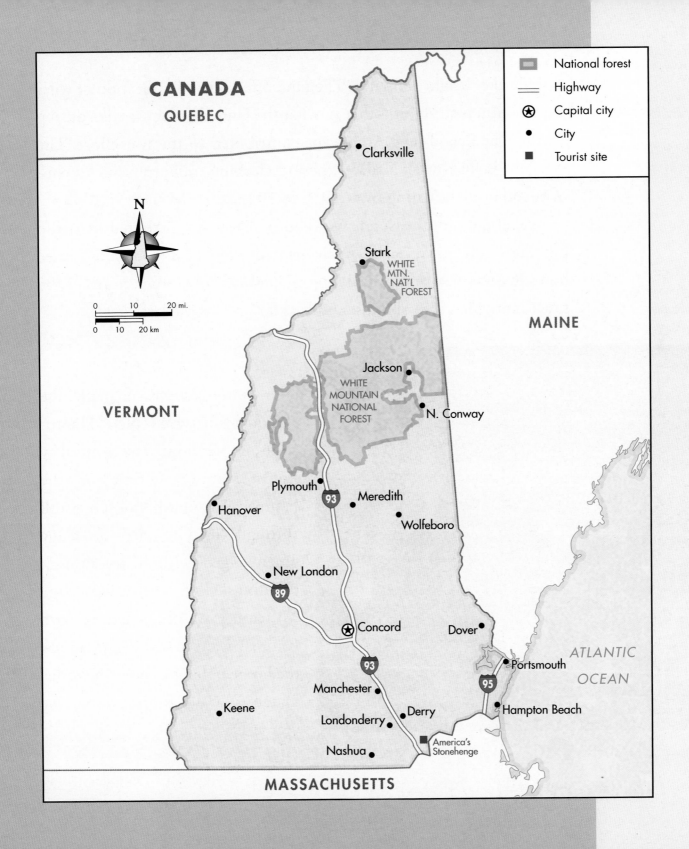

CANADA
QUEBEC

National forest
Highway
Capital city
City
Tourist site

• Clarksville

• Stark
WHITE MTN. NAT'L FOREST

MAINE

VERMONT

WHITE MOUNTAIN NATIONAL FOREST

• Jackson

• N. Conway

N

0   10   20 mi.
0   10   20 km

Plymouth •
93

• Meredith

• Hanover

• Wolfeboro

• New London
89

⊛ Concord

• Dover

ATLANTIC OCEAN

93

• Portsmouth

• Manchester

95

• Keene

• Derry

• Londonderry

• Hampton Beach

■ America's Stonehenge

• Nashua

MASSACHUSETTS

wall, it's the Wright Museum. The tank offers a good indication of what the museum is all about—that is, what the United States was like during World War II and how Americans contributed to the war effort. The museum is filled with artifacts, period clothing, military vehicles, and many other items dating from 1939 to 1945.

Wakefield, southeast of Wolfeboro, has many original, historic buildings in its town center. At the Museum of Childhood, you can see how children lived and played long ago. Wakefield Corner, north of the town center, has several houses built as far back as the late 1700s.

Dartmouth College is one of the leading universities in the United States.

The Connecticut River Valley

The Connecticut River marks the boundary between New Hampshire and Vermont. The river valley holds Hanover, home of the famous Dartmouth College. Stroll through town to view a village green edged with historic brick buildings. The Webster Cottage Museum is another Hanover site you may want to investigate. It was the home of famous political leader Daniel Webster during his senior year at Dartmouth.

The Monadnock Region

Towns in the Monadnock Region, in the southwestern corner of New Hampshire, are small. They are spread far apart over farmland and forest. Dotting the landscape are many small ponds and lakes.

The most-hiked peak in the world, rugged Mount Monadnock, is in this region. If you hike to the top of the mountain you'll be rewarded with a view of rolling hills, farmland, and forests. Also in this region is Keene, home of Keene State College. Keene is said to have the widest Main Street in the world. South of Keene is Swanzey, where you can see four covered bridges.

WALK YOUR HORSES OR PAY TWO DOLLARS FINE

EXTRA! EXTRA!

There are more than sixty covered bridges in New Hampshire. They all have a roof and wooden sides, but no two bridges are exactly alike. The size of the opening on the earliest bridges, built in the 1800s, was based on the height and width of a load of hay.

The White Mountain region is in north central New Hampshire. Tourists have enjoyed these huge granite peaks since the 1800s. Today, about six million visitors every year enjoy hiking, fishing, skiing, climbing, bird-watching, kayaking, camping, or snowmobiling in White Mountain National Forest. Nearby attractions include golfing, tax-free shopping, and live theater.

"The Old Man of the Mountain" is New Hampshire's official state symbol. It was a rock formation made up of five ledges that jutted out from Profile Mountain. In 2003, it collapsed and crashed to the ground below. A memorial is in the works.

In the summer, tourists hike the New Hampshire Heritage Trail or take bike trips. They also swim or canoe the Pemigewasset River or take a tour through the Polar Caves—a maze of crawl spaces through jumbled granite. In winter, skiers flock to Loon Mountain or Waterville Valley resort.

Great North Woods Region

North Country is the far frontier of hills, trees, and streams in northern New Hampshire. This wild backwoods is the place to go if you like to camp, hunt, fish, and snowmobile. Route 16 through the former mill town of Berlin is nicknamed "Moose Alley" for some of the four-legged traffic. At the Northern Forest Heritage Park you can learn how important the forest and the mill are to Berlin. The park also sponsors shows about New Hampshire's forest and rivers, a variety of concerts, and logging contests.

NEW HAMPSHIRE ALMANAC

Statehood date and number: June 21, 1788; ninth

State seal: The ship, *Raleigh*, in the center with a granite boulder, rising sun, and laurel wreath. The phrase, "Seal of the State of New Hampshire" surrounds the seal. Adopted in 1931.

State flag: Laurel leaves and nine stars surround the state seal upon a blue field. Adopted in 1909 and revised in 1931.

Geographic center: Belknap County, 3 miles (5 km) east of Ashland

Total area/rank: 9,350 square miles (24,216 sq km)/44th

Coastline: 18 miles (29 km)

Borders: Canada, Maine, Atlantic Ocean, Massachusetts, and Vermont

Latitude and longitude: Between 42°40' N and 48°18' N, longitude 70–37 W.

Highest/lowest elevation: Mount Washington, 6,288 feet (1,918 m) above sea level/sea level

Hottest/coldest temperature: 106°F (41°C) in 1911 at Nashua/–46°F (–43°C) in 1925 at Pittsburg

Land area/rank: 8,968 square miles (23,227 sq km)

Inland water area/rank: 314 square miles (813 sq km)

Population/rank (2005 census): 1,309,940/41st

Population of major cities:

Manchester: 107,006

Nashua: 86,605

Concord: 40,687

Derry: 34,021

Origin of state name: Named by John Mason after his home county of Hampshire, England

Capital: Concord (since 1808)

Previous capitals: The seat of government moved from Portsmouth to Exeter in 1776

Counties: 10

State government: 400 representatives, 24 senators

Major rivers/lakes: Connecticut River, Merrimack River, Piscataqua River, Androscoggin River, Saco River/Lake Winnipesaukee, Lake Squam, Lake Ossipee, Lake Sunapee, First Connecticut Lake, Second Connecticut Lake

Farm products: Hay, apples, milk, beef, eggs, chicken, hogs, sheep, turkeys, and blueberries

Livestock: Cattle, poultry, hogs

Manufactured products: Machinery and equipment, instruments, electronic equipment, rubber products, plastics, publishing, metal products, textiles and apparel, paper goods

Mining products: Sand, gravel, gemstones, and stone, including granite

Fishing products: Shrimp, cod, tuna, pollock, and lobster

Amphibian: Spotted newt

Animal: White-tailed deer

Bird: Purple finch

Butterfly: Karner blue

Emblem: Old Man of the Mountain, surrounded by the words "State of New Hampshire" and "Live Free or Die." Adopted 1945.

Gem: Smoky quartz

Flower: Purple lilac

Freshwater fish: Brook trout

Insect: Ladybug

Mineral: Beryl

Motto: "Live Free or Die"

Nicknames: Granite State, Mother of Rivers, White Mountain State, Switzerland of America

Rock: Granite

Saltwater game fish: Striped bass

Song: "Old New Hampshire" was officially adopted in 1949; words by John F. Holmes and music by Maurice Hoffmann Jr.

Sport: Skiing

Tree: White birch

Wildflower: Pink lady's slipper

Wildlife: Muskrat, white-tailed deer, beavers, porcupines, snowshoe hares, monarch butterflies, mockingbirds, cardinals, honeybees, black bears, moose, coyotes, shrews, voles, moles, raccoons, skunks, chipmunks, red squirrels, osprey, bald eagles, and trout

TIMELINE

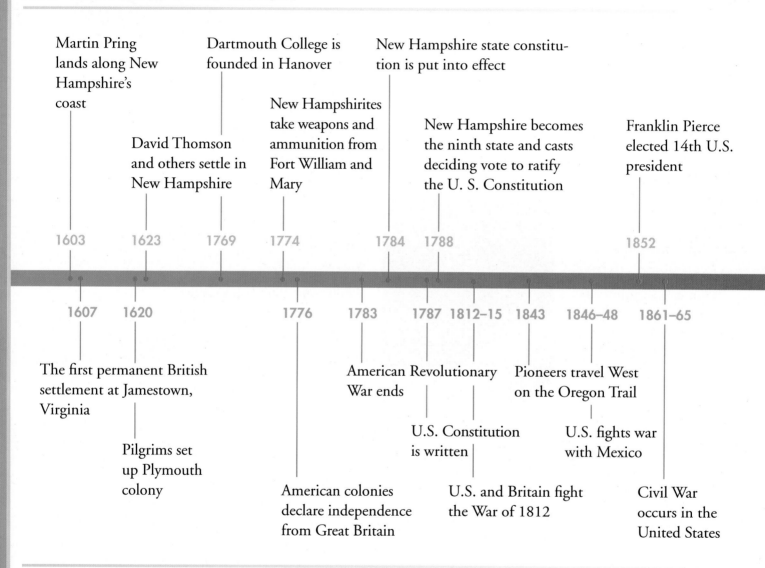

Martin Pring lands along New Hampshire's coast

David Thomson and others settle in New Hampshire

Dartmouth College is founded in Hanover

New Hampshirites take weapons and ammunition from Fort William and Mary

New Hampshire state constitution is put into effect

New Hampshire becomes the ninth state and casts deciding vote to ratify the U. S. Constitution

Franklin Pierce elected 14th U.S. president

1603   1623   1769   1774   1784 1788   1852

1607 1620   1776   1783   1787 1812–15 1843   1846–48   1861–65

The first permanent British settlement at Jamestown, Virginia

Pilgrims set up Plymouth colony

American Revolutionary War ends

Pioneers travel West on the Oregon Trail

U.S. Constitution is written

U.S. fights war with Mexico

American colonies declare independence from Great Britain

U.S. and Britain fight the War of 1812

Civil War occurs in the United States

UNITED STATES HISTORY

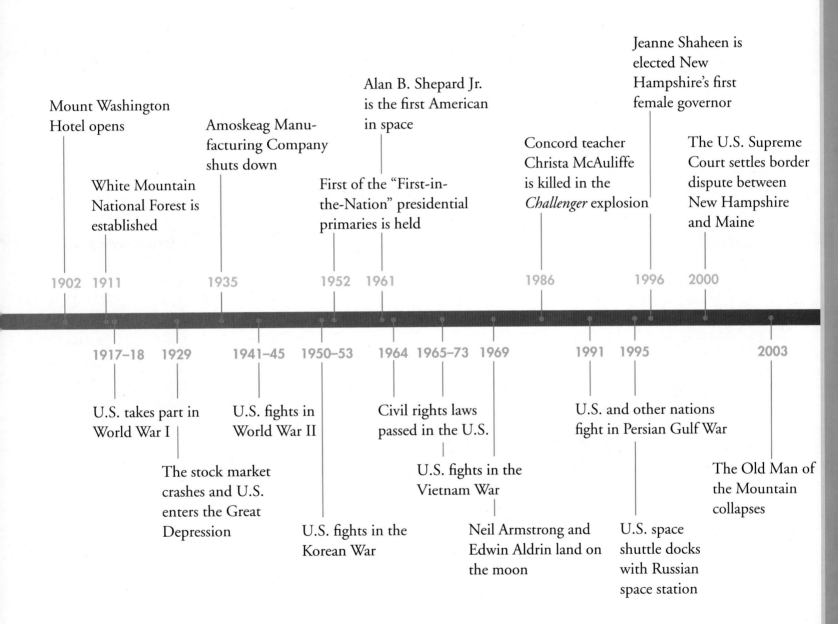

Mount Washington
Hotel opens

White Mountain
National Forest is
established

Amoskeag Manu-
facturing Company
shuts down

Alan B. Shepard Jr.
is the first American
in space

First of the "First-in-
the-Nation" presidential
primaries is held

Concord teacher
Christa McAuliffe
is killed in the
Challenger explosion

Jeanne Shaheen is
elected New
Hampshire's first
female governor

The U.S. Supreme
Court settles border
dispute between
New Hampshire
and Maine

1902   1911   1935   1952   1961   1986   1996   2000

1917–18   1929   1941–45   1950–53   1964   1965–73   1969   1991   1995   2003

U.S. takes part in
World War I

U.S. fights in
World War II

Civil rights laws
passed in the U.S.

U.S. and other nations
fight in Persian Gulf War

The stock market
crashes and U.S.
enters the Great
Depression

U.S. fights in the
Korean War

U.S. fights in the
Vietnam War

Neil Armstrong and
Edwin Aldrin land on
the moon

U.S. space
shuttle docks
with Russian
space station

The Old Man of
the Mountain
collapses

73

GALLERY OF FAMOUS NEW HAMPSHIRITES

Ken Burns
(1953–)
One of America's most well-known documentary film-makers. He has made movies on many subjects, including the Civil War, baseball, and jazz music. Lives in Walpole.

E. E. (Edward Estlin) Cummings
(1894–1962)
Noted poet and accomplished artist. Lived in Silver Lake.

Mary Baker Eddy
(1821–1910)
Author, publisher, and religious leader. She founded a religion called Christian Science, along with one of the most respected newspapers in the world, *The Christian Science Monitor.* Lived in Concord.

Robert Frost
(1874–1963)
One of America's leading 20th century poets and winner of four Pulitzer Prizes. Born in California and later lived in Derry.

Sarah Hale
(1788–1879)
Editor and writer. In the early 1800s she served as editor of a popular magazine, *Godey's Lady's Book.* She also wrote poetry, including the words to "Mary Had a Little Lamb," which was later set to music. Born in Newport.

Donald Hall
(1928–)
Prize-winning poet laureate of New Hampshire. He started writing at age twelve and has authored dozens of books of poetry. Lives in Wilmot.

John Irving
(1942–)
Well-known novelist. At least two of this author's books, including *The World According to Garp* and *The Cider House Rules,* have been made into movies. Born in Exeter.

J. D. (Jerome David) Salinger
(1919–)
Famous American novelist and short-story writer. His best-known work is *Catcher in the Rye.* He was born in New York City and lives in Cornish.

David H. Souter
(1939–)
A United States Supreme Court justice since 1990. Grew up in Weare.

GLOSSARY

ancient: having to do with times long ago

colony: a land or place settled by people from another country

conservation: careful use and maintenance of natural resources

constitution: the set of principles adopted by a state for its government

drumlin: a glacier-molded hill

elevation: height above sea level

erosion: wearing away of land by wind, water, or ice over a long period of time

erratic: a rock relocated by a glacier

estuary: the inland arm of a sea

granite: a very hard rock, usually gray or pink

kettle: a hole under a glacier that remains after the glacier has melted

marsh: low-lying land, usually wet

mast: a pole to support sails and rigging on a ship

nomad: a person with no permanent home

province: a region governed as part of a country

proximity: nearness in space

quarrying: the process of extracting stone from the land

textile: woven fabric

FOR MORE INFORMATION

Web sites

New Hampshire State Government Online
http://www.nh.gov/
Information about New Hampshire's government.

The Official Site of the New Hampshire Division of Travel and Tourism Development
http://www.visitnh.gov/
Facts about New Hampshire, as well as information on each of the regions in New Hampshire.

New Hampshire Almanac
http://www.nh.gov/nhinfo/index.html
A brief history of New Hampshire.

Books

Cherry, Lynne. *River Ran Wild: An Environmental History*. New York, NY: Harcourt Brace, 1992.

Cole, Michael D. *Challenger: America's Space Tragedy (Countdown to Space)*. Berkeley Heights, NJ: Enslow Publishers, 1995.

Marsh, Carole. *Yum, Yum!: The New Hampshire Kid's Cookbook*. Peachtree City, GA: Gallopade Pub Group, 1990.

Addresses

New Hampshire Historical Society
Tuck Library
30 Park Street
Concord, NH 03301-6394

State of New Hampshire
Office of the Governor
State House
25 Capitol Street
Concord, NH 03301

INDEX

ABOUT THE AUTHOR

Terry Miller Shannon writes fiction and nonfiction for readers of all ages. She loves to garden and walk along the beach with her husband, Craig, at their home in Gold Beach, Oregon. She wrote *New Hampshire* by reading books and doing research on the Internet.

Photographs © 2009: Bob LaPree Photography: 49, 70 top left; Corbis Images: 27, 39, 74 bottom left, 74 top left (Bettmann), 51 (Kevin Fleming), 54 (Dave G. Houser), 11 top (David Muench), 10, 11 bottom (Phil Schermeister), 74 top right (Marko Shark), 43, 67 (Lee Snider), 55 (Joseph Sohm/ChromoSohm), 71 left (Tim Zurowski), 18, 29 top, 37, 42; Dean Abramson: 60; Eric Poggenpohl: 64; Getty Images: 28, 63, 74 bottom right (Archive Photos), 3 left, 8 (Robert Bossi/Stone), 68 (Thomas J. Croke), 58 (Dan Gair), 29 bottom (Kean Collection/Archive Photos), 16 (Brian Smith); Kindra Clineff: 70 right; MapQuest.com, Inc.: 70 bottom left; New Hampshire Historical Society, Concord, NH/www.nhhistory.org: 21, 22 top, 25, 52; NH Stock Photography/John Gauvin: 62; North Wind Picture Archives: 19, 20, 22 bottom, 24, 26, 30, 32; Photo Researchers, NY: 3 right, 13 (Michael P. Gadomski), 15 (Lawrence Migdale); Richard T. Nowitz: 35; Robertstock.com: 4 (H. Abernathy), 7, 61 (F. Sieb), 71 right; Stock Montage, Inc.: 31, 34; The Image Works/Lee Snider: 48, 66; Transparencies Inc./Henryk T. Kaiser: cover; Visuals Unlimited: 41; Walter Bibikow: 9, 45, 50 background.